Janis Balodis was born in Australia of Latvian parents who settled in North Queensland after the Second World War. He trained and taught at E15 Acting School in London. His first play, *Backyard*, was workshopped at the Australian National Playwrights' Conference and produced by Nimrod Theatre in 1980. Other plays include *Happily Never After*, *Summerland*, *Heart for the Future* and *Double Take*. Music theatre works include *The Mercenary*, *Mr Barbeque*, *Electric Lenin* and *Red Cap*.

Currency Press has published *Wet and Dry* and, in 2006, *Perfect Skin*, his adaptation of Nick Earls' novel, as well *The Ghosts Trilogy*, premiered by the Melbourne Theatre Company, which comprises *Too Young for Ghosts*, *No Going Back* and *My Father's Father* and which draws on his Latvian heritage.

Balodis has also written for television and radio. He was an Associate Director of Melbourne Theatre Company (1988–93) and Dramaturg-in-Residence and Artistic Associate at Queensland Theatre Company (1995–96).

He currently lives on the North Coast of NSW.

Melanie Zanetti in the 2010 NORPA production.
(Photo: David Young)

ENGINE

a play by
JANIS BALODIS

CURRENCY PRESS
SYDNEY

CURRENCY TEENAGE SERIES

First published in 2011
by Currency Press Pty Ltd,
PO Box 2287, Strawberry Hills, NSW, 2012, Australia.
enquiries@currency.com.au
www.currency.com.au

NATIONAL LIBRARY OF AUSTRALIA CIP DATA

Author:	Balodis, Janis.
Title:	Engine / Janis Balodis
ISBN:	9780868198897 (pbk.)
Target Audience:	For secondary school age.
Dewey Number:	A822.3

Typeset for Currency Press by Dean Nottle.
Cover design by Emma Vine. Photograph by David Young.
Front cover shows Melanie Zanetti.

Australian Government

Australia Council
for the Arts

Publication of this title was
assisted by the Commonwealth
Government through the
Australia Council, its arts funding
and advisory body.

Contents

Currency Press acknowledges the Traditional Owners of the Country on which we live and work. We pay our respects to all Aboriginal and Torres Strait Islander Elders, past and present.

Introduction

Generator—powering shows that interact or connect

Julian Louis

In June 2006, the same week I accepted the job as Artistic Director at NORPA in Lismore, news headlines announced yet another carload of young people in a fatal car crash. The accident at Broken Head was horrific. It left little of the car and killed four boys from Kadina High School instantly. The driver survived, destined to live with the knowledge he had killed his mates. A close regional community struggled to come to terms with the loss and four families faced the future without a son.

So, while I celebrated my new job and new life, ten hours' drive north of Sydney my new community was in mourning.

In 2008 we launched a creative development program, NORPA Generator. Our first commission was *Engine*. Works created by a theatre company, particularly a regional company, need to reach out to the community in a variety of ways; they should reflect the culture in which they exist. *Engine* was a response to this community's experience of young people dying in cars—and to the families left behind. The concept of an interactive chorus was another way of connecting with our community while at the same time creating something highly theatrical—and it was an exciting challenge. Student performers from high schools across the northern rivers worked with us to develop these chorus scenes into something integral to the show.

Engine is a fictional work, but our starting point was a series of conversations with parents who had lost a son or daughter in a road crash—all on their personal journeys of pain and healing that probably continue today. In the course of this research we started to get a sense of the number of people directly affected by tragic road crashes. Janis wrote *Engine* using these and many other sources, including interviews with local mechanics. One of these, Matt Mason, we met regularly throughout the process, in his workshop. He would preach about how cars have evolved and become harder to 'feel'—they are automatic, lighter and faster, and the false confidence this instils in the young driver makes them 'deathtraps'. Getting your driver's licence is one of the few modern rights of passage. It's a grant of freedom but it comes at substantial risk—the more so as young people of every generation feel invincible.

The chorus were used primarily to create a heightened theatrical space within which they could comment or enlarge upon the emotional content of the play, such as when Grumps is trying not to think about what happened that night while the chorus perform his speculations at varying speeds. In the Lismore production, the chorus performed looped movements that could be interpreted as memories of, or nightmares about, what happened in the car. They become ghosts and friends left behind—and grease monkeys trying to help Tash finish building Stevie's car.

Making theatre regionally sometimes requires a tour if you want the play to 'run in'—otherwise the season can only last a week. So we designed a tour to Coffs Harbour, Murwillumbah, Lismore, Byron Bay, followed by three weeks in Brisbane at La Boite. This complicated our relationship to our school-student chorus, however, as they could not tour with us. We therefore created a number of choruses, working with nine schools and thirty student performers, each of which had to integrate with our touring cast of Bob Baines and Melanie Zanetti. To achieve this we created a 'rehearsal pack', which included workshop exercises and notes, the script and a fifty-minute DVD with scene-by-scene direction and physical-theatre tasks. Each of the groups then brought their own interpretation, words, movements and songs to the production. Our assistant director, Ajita Cannings, went into the schools to introduce the play and run workshops based on the rehearsal pack. When we met in the theatre we then incorporated their work into the production.

Janis has written *Engine* boldly yet with great sensitivity—as a father himself he seems to have captured the emotional landscape of loss and crisis within a close family. The characters' questions are unanswerable; in particular, 'What happened that night?' These scenes retrace the fatal steps towards 'that night'—they are moments of life on a loop that leave the family stuck, unable to go forward or back—even though, as Tom says in the play, 'It took three seconds'.

Engine is not a play about what happened or who to blame; it's about family and what we do to survive. Janis had managed to capture the thoughts of a family in grief, yet the tone at times is sharp, even tough. He doesn't dwell on the pain but rather on each character's fight with the grief and shock of losing Stevie.

Throughout the staging of *Engine* Janis gave me absolute trust and support. We enjoyed an inspiring collaboration, for which I thank him. There were many challenging aspects to this production apart from the chorus: we had a change of cast two weeks before opening night, not to mention the many cuts and changes we made on the road as we wound our way to Brisbane. The patience and skill of the cast, the technical team and the consistent enthusiasm of all the student performers made it all possible.

Something we heard many times from our audiences was that all kids should see this show. It's not a play that preaches but it is a warning—about the dangers of cars and the devastation they can cause.

Lismore, NSW

Julian's career has been influenced by work made with devising ensembles, by regional communities and by his training as an actor in London with Philippe Gaulier. He holds a BA degree in Communications, Theatre and Media from Bathurst and is also a NIDA director graduate. He is currently Artistic Director of NORPA (Northern Rivers Performing Arts) where he curates and creates new theatre.

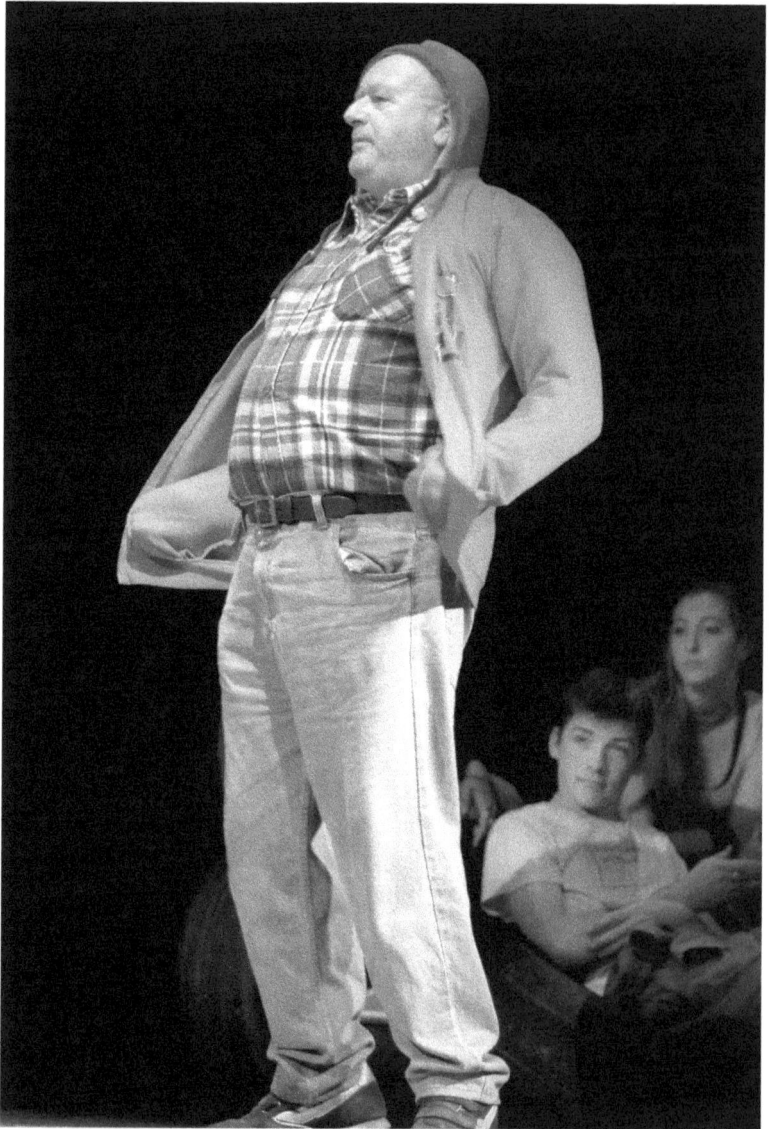

Bob Baines and Chorus in the 2010 NORPA production.
(Photo: David Young)

First Production

Engine was first produced by NORPA at Star Court Theatre, Lismore, NSW, on 29 July 2010, with the following cast:

Natasha   Melanie Zanetti
Grumpop   Bob Baines

Director, Julian Louis
Designer, Justin Nardella
Composer, Matt Hill

Characters

   Natasha, 17, (also known as Tash)
   Grumpop, 60, her grandfather (also known as Grumps and Pops)
   Mum (Emily), Natasha's and Stevie's mum
   Dad (Frank), Natasha's and Stevie's dad
   Stevie, Natasha's brother
   Davo, one of Stevie's friends
   Father Donovan, priest
   Politician
   Bob, a crash test dummy
   Larry, a crash test dummy
   Tom, the surviving driver
   Chorus / Kids in the car

The original production was performed with two actors playing multiple roles and a chorus of high school students who created their own choreography and some of their own text. The script was conceived and written with this minimal casting in mind. However, it would be possible to cast the play using more actors and doubling the roles in different combinations. These actors could also play the Chorus. Another option is that members of the Chorus play some of the other characters. A further option is that only two actors without a Chorus could perform the play. The exercise of these options or any others depends on availability of resources and on the experience of the cast, particularly of the Chorus.

The Chorus sequences are suggestions of how it may be involved in the action rather than a prescription. Again, the experience of the Chorus and the director will determine the nature and extent of their involvement. For example, a more experienced Chorus may facilitate scene and character changes.

The design of the play should allow fluid movement from scene to scene without much in the way of scene or costume changes. It seems self evident that the play features an actual engine prop. It is important that the engine be designed in such a way that the actors can work on it and attach various components, and finally, that it appears to start at the end of the play.

Approaching sounds of a revving car engine drawing nearer at speed.
The sound of the racing engine is accompanied by a driving music beat.
Headlights sweep through the darkness erratically.
The screech of tyres followed by a sickening, extremely loud thud.
Silence.
Only a tail-light glows dimly in the darkness.
The ticking of hot metal.
A mobile phone rings and rings.
Blackness.
The sound of a chain being pulled through a pulley.
An engine block (i.e. not complete) drops into the space on chains.
***CHORUS 1**: Four members of the CHORUS sit at the edges of the space, faces lit by their mobile phones. They look like ghosts as they send text messages. The scrolling letters appear garbled until they form into the first text message below.*
GRUMPOP and NATASHA. Night.

TEXT MESSAGE: Hug at own risk, may bite

Grumpop Any casseroles come today, Natasha?

Natasha No, Grumps, not that I noticed.

Grumpop Probably the end of them then.

Natasha Can't say I'm sad about that.

Grumpop Complete strangers turning up with casseroles. For a whole month.

Natasha Complete strangers wanting to hug you for a whole month.

Grumpop Lived in this town all my life and I didn't know half those people.

Natasha Other people's food just means something bad happened.

Grumpop Something bad happened.

Natasha I want our food.

Grumpop Your mum's been in no state to cook.

Natasha I'm over other people's food.

Grumpop You'll just have to put up with my cooking now the casseroles have stopped.

Natasha Does that mean you're moving in, Grumps?

Grumpop Till things get back on an even keel again.

Natasha So long as there's no hugging. I'm over being hugged too, Grumps. I'm over being told I'm brave. I'm over being told that whatever I do, whatever I say, whatever I feel is normal. I'm right over being normal. Even if I go mad people say it's normal—and then they try to hug you. How mad do you have to be before they stop?

Grumpop People you know forcing pills on you is not normal either.

Natasha You mean like Dad?

SCENE SHIFT

GRUMPOP and DAD.

One actor plays both GRUMPOP and DAD.

Grumpop I don't want pills, Frank. I don't need pills.

Dad In case you can't sleep, Pops.

Grumpop Who can sleep? Can you sleep?

Dad The doctor said. In case.

Grumpop No-one can sleep, Frank.

Dad That's the point. Em needs them.

Grumpop Do they work?

Dad I'm taking them. He gave me some pills for you too.

Grumpop When I need something that bad, Frank, I'm not taking it. Can't be good for you.

Dad Suit yourself, Pops. No-one's forcing you. They're here if you need them.

DAD leaves a small receptacle of pills.

SCENE SHIFT

GRUMPOP and NATASHA.

Grumpop Got some for you too, Natasha?

Natasha Yeah, but I'm not taking them. I want to know what's going on.

Grumpop I know you're not sleeping.

2

Natasha I don't need pills. I want to be able to get out of the way of the next hugger.

Grumpop Wandering round the garage all hours of the night. Thought I was seeing a ghost.

Natasha When?

Grumpop Thought it was Stevie. Coming home late, like he used to. I almost had a go at him.

Natasha Do you really think he's still here?

Grumpop I realised it was you wearing some of Stevie's clothes.

Natasha Don't tell Mum. She doesn't want his room touched. Nothing moved. Sometimes she just stands in there. For ages.

Grumpop Your dad told me.

Natasha In the middle of his room. Or she lies on his bed hugging his doona.

SCENE SHIFT

NATASHA becomes her MUM standing in Stevie's room.

MUM stands stock still. As though listening for him. There is a doona hanging in the space. And a pillow on the floor.

GRUMPOP becomes DAD. He notices her and watches from the doorway. He goes to move away but changes his mind.

Dad Emily? Em.

> *When she doesn't respond he moves to stand in front of her. She still doesn't acknowledge his presence or move.*

Emily. Sweetheart.

> *He reaches out to her and she flinches slightly from his touch, stopping him.*

Mum I think if I listen for him, really listen, Stevie will be here.

Dad I wish Stevie was here too, Em. I brought your pill.

> *She takes the pill automatically, goes to the doona and embraces it, breathing in its smell. DAD takes hold of the doona, gently trying to take it from her. A silent but intense struggle. She wraps it around her and then she's gone. DAD picks up the pillow and inhales its smell.*

3

SCENE SHIFT

GRUMPOP and NATASHA.

Natasha They fight over who gets the doona you know. The loser gets the pillow.

Grumpop The first night I saw you down here I was hoping it was Stevie.

Natasha I always put his clothes back in the morning before Mum gets up.

Grumpop Or his ghost. I'd settle for that. I've gone off being normal too.

Natasha He's here you know. I can feel him. This is the only place.

SCENE SHIFT

NATASHA alone. She cuts her arms with an old Stanley knife.

Natasha I talk to you, Stevie, and you're far, far away. I thought if I could talk to you it'd be like I'm with you, like you're there— not here, no—but there. [*Cutting herself*] Just there. [*Cutting herself*] Just there. [*Cutting herself*] Just trying to feel something. Anything. I can't talk to you as if you aren't ever coming back. I started sending you text messages. Not started. Never really stopped. Even that night when I heard there'd been a crash. Stupid things. Watcha doin'? Watcha doin'? Like we used… like forever.

TEXT MESSAGE Going down where it happened.

Natasha There's a bunch going down from school. Your mates. Probably kids I don't even know. It's a month. And none of us has been there. Not Mum, not Dad, not Grumps. Not me. I don't want to go. I do but I don't. I have to. Davo is taking me.

TEXT MESSAGE C U there.

SCENE SHIFT

GRUMPOP becomes DAVO.
NATASHA at a roadside shrine. Three crosses. Flowers and cards attached to them. More flowers at their bases. DAVO is there with her.

Music from an iPod with speakers or as though from a car stereo, heavy on the bass.

CHORUS 2: *A simple ritual which involves: arrival of four CHORUS members, the placement of tokens and flowers, a photo of Stevie. Their reactions on arrival involve speculation on what they think happened or rumours of what they heard had happened. Three or four statements such as: 'I heard they were dragging another car', 'Yeah, they reckon the tyres weren't fitted right'. This speculation stops on NATASHA's arrival.*

A CHORUS member or whole group may arrive singing an appropriate song.

They might take photos of the shrine with their phones.

TEXT MESSAGES Miss you S- man. Hope your in a good place. Love you Stevie. Always here for you Pete

      NATASHA is standing with DAVO. He's a bit awkward.

Davo Do you want to be alone for a bit?

Natasha No, Davo.

Davo You alright?

Natasha Don't know what I was expecting.

Davo I can wait in the car.

Natasha Have you been out here before?

Davo The next day. All this was already… Like magic. No-one around. Bang! Not bang… Weird. You never see anyone. A whole lot of us came down after the funeral. All Stevie's mates. And Pete's. Simmo's. I still come by, maybe once a week, used to be more.

Natasha Why, Davo?

Davo Why? Come on, Tash?

Natasha No, I really want to know.

Davo Stevie was a mate. Pete too. Best mates. It's what you do. Why we all came down here.

Natasha Do you think… Stevie and Pete, Simmo… they're still here?

Davo I don't know. Maybe. Kind of.

Natasha And they'll always be here?

Davo Yeah, kind of. What I felt the next day. Maybe… what I wanted to feel. But no, I hope not.

Natasha What about now? Today?

Davo I don't stop much anymore. I used to. Every time. Not anymore.

Natasha It's not what you want to remember.

Davo But it's something you never want to forget.

Natasha You're a good friend, Davo.

Davo Not good enough. I could have given Stevie a lift home that night too, when he asked me to take you.

Natasha He went with Tom.

Davo Yeah, but I never even asked him.

> *CHORUS 2A: One CHORUS member stands and puts his arm in a sling. It's as though Tom has arrived. The others look at him.*

Natasha He wanted to go with Tom.

Davo Tom's still alright, eh?

Natasha Is he?

Davo Hardly a scratch. Stevie and Pete and Simmo…

Natasha What happened in the car? Somebody must know.

Davo Tom. He's still alive. But he won't say anything.

Natasha I heard he can't remember.

Davo Not what I heard. His parents, the lawyers won't let him. Told him not to when he was in hospital. Say nothing. Because the cops are out to get him. Hope they nail him good.

> *He's gone.*

Natasha Stevie? I thought I'd—feel you. I sent you a text that night soon as I heard. [*Checking her phone*] It's still here. I can send it again.

TEXT MESSAGE Come home Stevie please come home.

SCENE SHIFT

GRUMPOP and NATASHA. Garage.

Grumpop You've been down here more nights lately. Sleeping in his car.

Natasha I can't sleep upstairs.

Grumpop You can't keep sleeping in the car.

Natasha I can't stand listening to Dad cry himself to sleep when there's nothing anyone can do about it. Nothing I can do about it.

6

Grumpop I'm getting rid of it.

Natasha What?

Grumpop That's when this trouble started.

Natasha What trouble? Stevie wasn't driving. It wasn't his car.

Grumpop I should've—known it'd end in tears

Natasha It was Tom's car.

Grumpop Doesn't matter whose car. I told him and told him.

Natasha Told him what?

Grumpop In the wrong hands a car's a weapon. A lethal weapon.

Natasha Tom was driving.

Grumpop Biggest mistake of my life—helping Stevie get this car.

Natasha You can't blame Stevie's car. It isn't even going. He never got to finish it.

Grumpop That's all over with. It's out of here. We've all got to work harder at keeping our shit together. Leaving his stuff hanging round won't help. Get back to sleeping in bed, practising the piano… doing your schoolwork.

Natasha Just leave his car alone. It's not hurting you.

Grumpop It's a sad bloody reminder. Every bloody day.

Natasha Mum won't let you.

Grumpop She won't be too keen on you getting round in his clothes and sleeping in his car either.

Natasha Don't you tell me what I can and fucking can't do. Just don't touch his car. Stay away from it if it freaks you out. Take some fucking pills.

Grumpop You never used to have a tongue on you. Only goes to prove my point. We're going to have to learn how to behave like civilised human beings all over again.

Natasha Maybe you can start by minding your own business. That car now belongs to me.

SCENE SHIFT

NATASHA is lighting a candle in church.

GRUMPOP becomes FATHER DONOVAN.

CHORUS 3: *CHORUS members also light candles and arrive during the monologue. They remain present as ghostly witnesses until the end of the scene*

TEXT MESSAGE In the dark the monster comes.

Natasha I'm lighting a candle for you, Stevie, whatever good that is. Skipping class. I can't see a reason to do maths. I know it was your favourite subject but what's the point of exams now? How many times in life does anyone use the word hypotenuse? 'Oh, what a lovely hypotenuse your roof makes.' [*Lighting another candle*] Do people light a candle instead of praying? Because they can't pray? I remember, Stevie, when we were kids, at night, alone in the dark, you used to light a candle to stop the monster coming. I asked how you knew it worked and you said it must because the monster didn't come. Lucky we didn't burn the house down. [*Lighting another candle*] I need you to light a candle for me now, Stevie. The monster is always in the dark again now. I should be telling you about school but I've missed a fair bit. Apparently that's normal. I had a big row with Grumps, over your car. I swore at him. That's probably normal too, but he didn't seem to think so. Maybe we should both be on the pills like Mum and Dad, not that it seems to do them any good. [*She holds her hand in the flame of a candle.*] I thought I would be able to feel you in here. Nothing. [*Lighting another candle*] I suppose this light is meant to represent the soul. Such a sad little light, with a little tear of wax running down the side. Is that why people light candles, so they'll do their crying for them? [*She deliberately drips some hot wax on herself.*] Not much point in lighting just one then, is there?

> *She lights more and more candles.*
> *FATHER DONOVAN appears at the other end of the church aisle, watches her for a moment.*

Father Donovan You, girl! Stop! What the flaming blazes do you think you are up to? Are you trying to set the place on fire?

Natasha Sorry, Father.

Father Donovan Oh, it's you. Natasha.

Natasha I'll pay for them, Father.

Father Donovan No, no it's not about the money.

Natasha I was lighting a candle for Stevie's soul. I guess I got carried away.

Father Donovan He had a big soul, did Stevie. One candle wouldn't be enough.

Natasha Well, I suppose that's normal under the circumstances.

Father Donovan For arsonists maybe. I can't say I've encountered it before.

Natasha Oh, sorry then, Father. I better be getting back to class.

Father Donovan Haven't seen you at church lately, Natasha.

Natasha It doesn't work for me anymore, Father. I can't pray. I don't know how to do that. Whatever I would ask God for, God isn't going to give me.

Father Donovan You can't avoid God, Natasha, by not coming in to the church. God is out there as well.

Natasha Where's Stevie now, Father? And Pete? / With Go—?

Father Donovan With God, from whence they came.

Natasha You know why I don't come to church? People come up to me and they tell me how beautiful the service was. Maybe it was. I don't know. I don't remember. A beautiful funeral. Like Stevie and Pete wouldn't rather still be here. How fucked is that? Sorry, Father.

Father Donovan No you're not.

Natasha You're right. It's getting to be a habit. I could have said how messed up is that.

Father Donovan I'd bet it was his friends that come and say those things to you.

Natasha Yeah.

Father Donovan Good friends.

Natasha I suppose. Mostly.

Father Donovan They're grieving too, as best they can, letting you know they care. You can tell a lot about a person by their friends. And whether or not they'll burn the church down lighting candles to you.

Natasha It's no good. He's not here, you know. The only place I can feel where Stevie is, is in his car. It's mostly in bits. How normal is that?

Father Donovan For petrol-heads maybe.

Natasha Stevie loved his car.

Father Donovan And you love him. Try praying there. You can pray any place feels right. God doesn't care.

Natasha Don't you?

Father Donovan Promise me I'll see you in here again, without needing a fire extinguisher.

9

Natasha I can't say when.

Father Donovan God bless you, Natasha.

Natasha [*automatically*] And you, Father.

Father Donovan Gotcha.

Natasha See you, Father.

Father Donovan How is your mother?

Natasha I think she does her praying in Stevie's room.

Father Donovan Tell her I'll come by and see her.

CHORUS has also gone, leaving their lit candles.

SCENE SHIFT

NATASHA becomes MUM in Stevie's room at night.

Mum Is now the worst time? I feel I'm walking on ice so thin it cracks beneath my feet and I'll never reach the shore. I'm stuck here, between worlds. I know the past. You're in it, remembered. Always there, in the photos, in the memories, forever with us. It's the future that's frightening, always the same. You're not there. When we eat dinner you are not there. When we watch TV together you are not there. When we are all in the car you're not there. This is our life now. Nothing is going to change. There won't be a phone call to say you're on your way home now. We won't wake up tomorrow and find you wandering out of the bathroom. We won't hear you singing to yourself, 'Watcha doin'? Watcha doin'?' Everything reminds me. You are not there. It's worse now than before. If there is worse to come I don't know how I will go on.

SCENE SHIFT

TEXT MESSAGE Better than new

NATASHA in the garage.

She noisily sorts through the toolbox, drops what she's carrying. The sound of metal falling on a concrete floor.

GRUMPOP appears, woken from sleep. Turns on fluoros, sees the lit candles everywhere.

Grumpop How is a man supposed to sleep? Tash, what the bloody hell are you doing?

Natasha Wish I knew.

Grumpop Put those bloody candles out before we all go up in smoke.

He begins to put the candles out and she tries to stop him. He wrestles his way around her, snuffing them out one by one.

Natasha No, leave them.

Grumpop You're losing your marbles, girl.

Natasha Stop. I said don't.

Grumpop Having a Viking funeral now, are we?

Natasha I lit them for Stevie.

Grumpop Sending him off in a burning car instead of a boat? You know what cars run on?

Natasha You're a real bastard, you know that?

Grumpop Same stuff we wash engine parts with, and wipe with rags filled with petrol and oil. And there's kero. Add your dad's paint tins and thinners and we got a regular time bomb here just waiting for some idiot to light the wick.

NATASHA only gets to put out one or two candles as he has pinched out all the others.

Natasha You could have just told me.

Grumpop Christ, Natasha, you've got a brain in your head. Used to be a good one.

Natasha I want to finish off Stevie's car.

Grumpop Setting it on fire will get it done real quick.

Natasha You know what I mean.

Pause.

Grumpop Do it during the day. I'm trying to sleep at night and I don't want to have to take the pills.

Natasha You could help me.

Grumpop Why the hell would I do that?

Natasha Why not?

Grumpop Finishing his car won't bring Stevie back.

Natasha I know that.

Grumpop What do you think you'd be doing?

Natasha I'd be learning about cars. Like Stevie.

Grumpop Why now? You've never shown the least bit of interest before. At least Stevie was into cars.

Natasha Because that's what you always talked to him about. Aren't girls supposed to know about cars?

Grumpop Not this one. I don't even want it here.

Natasha You could just tell me what to do.

Grumpop What's the difference? I might as well be doing it.

Natasha You used to help Stevie. You used to tell Stevie he had to know everything.

SCENE SHIFT

GRUMPOP and STEVIE.

NATASHA becomes STEVIE from a time when he was working on the car with GRUMPOP.

Grumpop Don't arse about, Stevie. If you're going to do it, do it right.

Stevie It wasn't my idea to pull the thing to bits.

Grumpop In my day if you wanted to master a machine you had to know how it worked.

Stevie It was working just fine. The engine wasn't even burning oil. Whatever happened to 'if it ain't broke—don't fix it'?

Grumpop It was leaking oil. The car is almost as old as you.

Stevie Yeah, well I ain't broke yet either.

Grumpop If it breaks when you're driving it, it'll be too late. A car is a weapon. A lethal weapon. You've got to know what it can and can't do. And what you can and can't do. Then maybe you won't be so quick to pull the trigger.

> *STEVIE has heard this so many times he mouths the words and mimes shooting himself in the head with a pistol.*

Mightn't be you. Mightn't be so lucky. Might be someone else. You don't need my help to be a smartarse, Stevie.

Stevie Okay, Grumps. Keep your hair shirt on. We'll make it good as new.

Grumpop You know how your car works, get everything up to standard, learn to respect it. Might actually save your life.

Stevie What if we make it better than new, Grumps?

Grumpop What, hot it up? It already has more power than you need.

Stevie But wouldn't it go even better?

Grumpop Just get this done. Learn this first. After that you can
have as much fancy chrome as you like. But you'll be on your own.

Stevie I'm pretty much doing it on my own now.

Grumpop If you put in the time, rather than riding round in some of
those deathtraps with your mates.

Stevie Yeah, yeah.

SCENE SHIFT

GRUMPOP and NATASHA.

STEVIE reverts back to NATASHA and the present.

Grumpop Look where it got him. Got us all.

Natasha That's not fair.

Grumpop If the world was in any ways fair, Stevie would be here
finishing that engine.

Natasha Is it because I'm a girl?

Grumpop It's not a girl thing, Tash.

Natasha It's what Stevie would have wanted.

Grumpop It's what he wanted. And if he'd finished it he wouldn't
have been in that other car. But he was. And now it's over.

Natasha I'm going to do it anyway.

Grumpop You go for it, for all your worth. I won't get in your way.
Just try and keep the noise down.

     He starts to go.

Natasha He's here you know.

Grumpop No. It's time you stopped thinking that. Stevie's not here.

Natasha That engine, his car, that's as much him as… as…

Grumpop Sadly, we both know it's not.

Natasha I'm asking you, Grumpop.

Grumpop Not even if you call me a bastard.

Natasha Please. For Stevie.

Grumpop You think I don't know I'm the one who got him fired
up about cars? You think I don't know I could have just fixed it
up and made it safe for him to drive? You think now I could just
finish it and pretend nothing happened?

Natasha For me then.

Grumpop I can't, Tash. I just can't.

SCENE SHIFT

TEXT MESSAGE Beware the mighty python!

NATASHA becomes MUM. GRUMPOP becomes DAD.

In this scene NATASHA switches between playing herself and her MUM.

Mum Natasha, Pops just told us that you're planning to work on… the car.

Natasha Was that a joke?

> *A look between MUM and DAD.*

Dad No, sweetie. Why would Pops joke about that?

Natasha 'Cause he knows I don't know what to do.

Dad Oh, well then…

Mum You could always ask your father.

Dad I suppose I could always ask Pops.

Mum You heard him say he refused to help, Tash. That's the reason he was telling us.

Dad Oh, well then… Too bad I don't know anything about cars. It's a wonder Pops let me marry you.

> *Pause.*

Mum You should have come with us, Tash.

Dad Group counselling. You would've loved it.

Natasha Was there hugging?

Mum Yes, quite a bit.

Natasha No thanks.

Dad It was our first time. We're group counselling virgins.

Mum That's what someone called us when we had tea and biscuits.

Dad Like we were being welcomed into a club.

Mum A club that no-one wants to join.

Natasha Did it help?

Dad What do you reckon?

Mum It was one of the strangest nights of my life.

Dad Like being trapped in a Monty Python sketch.

Natasha Monty Python?

Dad Yeah, you know, 'You were lucky. We lived in shoebox in middle of road and ate lumps of coal…' That sort of thing.

Natasha I don't get it.

Dad A sort of a competition. Who had suffered the most.

Mum A suffer-a-thon.

Dad You know, going round the circle taking it in turns. 'We lost Mum when she went to put in her Lotto tickets. Her number came up first.'

Mum 'She were lucky. At least it were quick.'

Dad 'Lucky? God took her before she could buy her ticket. She had the winning numbers. She weren't having a good week.'

Mum 'At least your mother didn't have to suffer. When my mother had cancer it was like she was slowly being eaten by a pack of lobsters after she'd been staked out on the beach with barbed wire at low tide.'

Dad 'Barbed wire is for babies. My poor old dad was pining for a blanket knitted out of barbed wire. He had the twitches so bad you'd think he was lying in a bed of broken glass with a box of wild bees on his head. Poor old bugger minced himself to death. We had to stop the cat eating him.'

Mum Stevie used to love Monty Python.

Dad He could rattle off whole sketches.

Natasha When it was your turn, what'd you say?

Dad Your mum got the giggles.

Mum It was terrible. I couldn't stop.

Dad Disgraced herself.

Natasha Mum, what'd you do?

Dad I saved her with a massive coughing fit.

Mum That just made it worse. I had to leave.

Dad We couldn't compete.

Natasha What are you supposed to get out of it?

Dad Comfort? Misery loves company.

Mum I'm going upstairs.

Dad I won't be long.

Mum There's no comfort in other people's suffering.

Dad We don't have to go again.

Mum 'Night, Natasha. Remember you've got school tomorrow.

Natasha 'Night, Mum.

MUM goes.
A silence between NATASHA and DAD.

Dad So.

Natasha So.

Dad It was good for your mum to have a laugh.

Natasha Yeah.

Dad First laugh in a while.

Natasha Mum loves Monty Python too.

Dad I think she feels guilty about laughing. Not about the others. Stevie. How are you, Tash?

Natasha [*with a shrug*] You know. Okay enough.

Dad So Pops said no.

Natasha Does that surprise you?

Dad He's your mum's dad and he always thought I was a hopeless prospect because I knew nothing about cars. I'm sorry.

Natasha There's always Google.

Dad Can you re-build a car with Google?

Natasha Can't see why not.

Dad Oh, well then—

Natasha Unless Mum wouldn't let me. 'Cause she wants nothing changed.

Dad Wouldn't you be better off getting back to your schoolwork? I know you haven't been doing much lately. And the school's been good about it. But—

Natasha We have to move on now. Get on with life.

Dad I was going to say you used to hate getting behind at school, even missing a day.

Natasha Everything's different now.

Dad For us. It's still the same for everyone else and we have to fit in.

Natasha I'm not a kid anymore. I've got more going on than the HSC.

Dad We don't want you throwing your life away.

Natasha That's the least of my problems.

Dad I know how you feel, Tash—

Natasha You have no idea. Who says I have to do the HSC next year? Does it matter when? I'll do it, alright?

Dad Your mum's going to notice if you're staying home every day to work on the car.

Natasha You're not letting things stay the same. You're always on the phone or catching a plane to talk to some politician or journalist about changing the law.

16

Dad I can't waste Stevie's life and do nothing.

Natasha That's why I want to finish his car.

Dad Pop told your mum we should… move it on. As is.

Natasha Did Mum say yes?

Dad She didn't say no.

Natasha Do you want to sell it?

Dad We'd like for things to stay just as they for the moment, without you stirring Pops up or your mum. Then later… What are you up to, Tash? Do you need to talk to someone… else?

Natasha Why? Don't you trust me?

Dad We'd like it if you were to keep going to school.

Natasha There was a call when you were out. Someone who works for the Minister for Roads.

Dad The pity is that Stevie had to die to get me off my arse.

SCENE SHIFT

DAD on the phone to a POLITICIAN.

CHORUS 4: The CHORUS members take it in turns to play the POLITICIAN, sharing out the lines, playing off each other, passing the phone. There are elements of mimicry and mockery in their delivery and it has the energy of kids trying to impress each other with their outrageousness. A rhythmic beat could accompany this scene and their text is delivered rhythmically.

Dad Did you read that essay I sent you by Christopher Lennings?

Politician / Chorus I'm sorry/ on my desk/ so sorry/ if you could tell me—

Dad You need to read it for yourself or you'll think I'm just another grief-stricken parent trying to make sense of why his kid was smashed up on the roads—

Politician / Chorus I'm sorry/ this must be difficult/ terribly painful/ I'm truly sorry.

Dad But this is not about me. It's about ten seconds of stupidity. Less. Three seconds.

Politician / Chorus Oh yes, it happens quickly/ three seconds/ two seconds/ one.

Dad Science was wrong about the male brain being fully developed at age fifteen. It's not fully developed till twenty-five…

17

Politician / Chorus There would be politicians/ of fifty-five/ whose brains don't function.

Dad Okay, not in some politicians. Anyway, that's why young men have trouble controlling impulses, why they do stupid things, why they think they're bulletproof.

Politician / Chorus Impulsive/ stupid/ bulletproof/ that's why we can send them off to war.

Dad We've got laws that say you have to do seven hours of theory to pull a beer but none, zero hours of theory to drive a car...

Politician / Chorus Seven hours/ to pull a beer/ a decent beer/ no, can't be done.

Dad If it takes one hundred hours of practice to pull a decent beer, and only three seconds to crash a car, why not make it one hundred and twenty hours on Ls to learn to drive safely?

Politician / Chorus Hundred twenty hours/ on your Ls/ to learn to drive/ parents won't buy it.

Dad A kid of sixteen does a written test, we give them their Ls. They can't drive but we give them a key. They stick it in a car, and hit the road.

Politician / Chorus Kids don't vote/ their parents do.

Dad At least a motorcycle rider has to do a weekend course. Who's more stupid, them or me and you?

Politician / Chorus Accidents happen/ no-one's stupid/ one percent/ of road accidents/ end in death/ dead/ dead/ dead/ I had an airbag.

Dad My son is one of the one percent who ended up dead. And you consider that an intelligent comment? Because so far you've dodged a bullet?

Politician / Chorus Sorry/ sorry/ that was stupid/ stupid/ please forgive me,

Dad Something you should know, I'm not going away. I'll come down to see you and I'll bring journalists. Repeat your comment to them.

Politician / Chorus Apologise/ was a stupid/ stupid thing to say/ I get your point.

Dad If you do, the one percent is something you can change. If you have two kids in a car, how many can die? If you have five kids in a car, how many can die? So how many could you save, with the stroke of your pen?

Politician / Chorus Two kids in the car/ how many die/ five kids in the car/ how many die/ you, you and you walk home/ what about you/ you could walk too/ I've got an airbag/ come on let's go/ go/ go/ I have to go.

Dad Think about it. Thanks for your time. And read the Lennings. [*He hangs up.*] A paper should be written on the brain development of politicians. It'd only be a short one.

> *DAD stands there, exhausted.*

SCENE SHIFT

NATASHA becomes MUM. She gives DAD a hug from behind.
They stand like that for a while. Still. Silent.

Mum What did you say to Natasha?

Dad That we'd like her to keep going to school.

> *They separate. Just standing. Still. Silent. They each pop a pill.*

Do you think these pills work?

Mum Are they supposed to make us happier?

Dad I don't think so.

Mum They're working then.

Dad Dr Taylor put us on the lowest dose. In case we become zombies.

Mum Wouldn't that be better?

Dad I can't tell if they have any effect or not.

Mum Do you want to go back and see the psychiatrist?

Dad No, do you?

Mum No. What can a psychiatrist do that would make things any better?

Dad Perhaps the pills slow things down. Like a brake.

> *MUM goes to the doona and embraces it, breathing in its smell. DAD takes hold of the doona, gently trying to take it from her.*

Emily. Emily.

> *A silent but intense struggle. She lets him have the doona. He tries to give it back to her.*

Mum I'm going to wait up for a while. If Stevie could find a way to come to me I know he would.

19

MUM stands alone in Stevie's room. As though listening for him.
She spits out the pill and puts it back into a small pill receptacle.

SCENE SHIFT

MUM and STEVIE.

STEVIE is trying to sneak out late at night.

Mum Stevie?
Stevie Boo!
Mum Stevie. What are you doing?
Stevie Sprung!
Mum I thought you were going to study and then go to bed.
Stevie I was studying.
Mum And?
Stevie I thought I'd go out for a bit.
Mum For a walk? I might come with you.
Stevie Mum.
Mum What?
Stevie Not for a walk.
Mum Oh.
Stevie I'm meeting some of the guys.
Mum Oh.
Stevie We're going for a drive.
Mum Oh.
Stevie Mum, don't keep saying 'Oh' like that.
Mum You know I don't like you doing this, Stevie.
Stevie I've been studying. I feel like my head is going to explode. I
    need some air. It's just a drive.
Mum Who's going?
Stevie Tom, Pete, maybe Simmo. Maybe not Stevie.
Mum Do you have a girlfriend, Stevie?
Stevie What?
Mum I just wondered if you had a girlfriend you hadn't mentioned.
Stevie I'm not sneaking over to some girl's place to…
Mum Oh. No, I didn't mean… it's none of my business.
Stevie Oh, do you think I'm gay?
Mum No.
Stevie Because I mostly go out with the boys?

Mum Are you?

Stevie Would it matter?

Mum No.

Stevie I'm not gay, Mum.

Mum It'd just be nice.

Stevie If I was?

Mum If you had a girlfriend.

Stevie She might stop me studying.

Mum That wouldn't be so good.

Stevie Mum, what's this about?

Mum I just want you to be happy.

Stevie I'm happy, okay?

Mum Okay.

Stevie Look, if I'm going to go then… the sooner I'll be back.

Mum Just this once.

Stevie What if I get a girlfriend?

Mum Don't push your luck, buster. And don't be late.

Stevie I promise.

He gives her a kiss on the cheek. Goes.

Mum I love you, Stevie.

Stevie I know, Mum. Don't wait up, okay.

Mum You know I will.

Stevie I'm happy, okay? [*Laughing*] I'm happy.

SCENE SHIFT

TEXT MESSAGE In space no-one can hear you scream

NATASHA alone, cutting herself with the Stanley knife. A quiet ritual.

CHORUS 5: CHORUS bring on tyres and arrange them to create seats in a car. One has an extension lead for the interior light. NATASHA goes and sits in the car with them. They watch her and may mirror her actions or cry like MUM.

Natasha Mum's in your room. Waiting. For you. Dad cried himself to sleep on your doona. They're still on the pills. Grumps has moved into the granny flat. Granddad flat I suppose it is now. He's splashing on more aftershave than usual because he thinks nobody knows he's on the whiskey. Unless he's drinking his

21

aftershave now. If he was in a cartoon they'd draw him in a cloud. Me, I'm normal, more normal than ever, which isn't quite as normal as you'd think. I stood at your door watching Mum. She didn't see me. I wanted to go in to her but I can't go in your room now. You know how Mum cries. Used to be a joke. We'd be watching movies on the tele, *Sleepless in Seattle* or something, and she'd be crying and we wouldn't even know. Tears running down her face. Completely silent. She could cry a lake and no-one would know till their feet got wet. Now it's a terrible silence. Just weird. [*She looks at the blood.*] I don't cry anymore. I want to be like Sylvia Plath, the poet. She would throw the furniture about and ended up with her head in the oven. If I was institutionalised I could just lie around and do nothing and be crazy. But apparently it's normal to feel like that.

Melanie Zanetti and Chorus in the 2010 NORPA production.
(Photo: David Young)

SCENE SHIFT

TEXT MESSAGE I hate you I hateyou ihateyouihateyuteuh8uh8uh8u

NATASHA in the garage, smashing everything in sight.

GRUMPOP comes to see what's going on. At first he doesn't try to stop her.

She sees him and defiantly continues on her wrecking path.

He tries to stop her but she dodges away and throws stuff in his direction so that he has to avoid being hit.

He joins in emptying toolboxes of spanners.

It's as though she only realises what she has done once he starts doing it.

She stops first.

CHORUS 6: *The CHORUS members, unseen by NATASHA and GRUMPOP, spin hubcaps into the space, and car parts which they leave lying about in the space, creating the impression of an 'exploded' car. The CHORUS sit in the tyres to witness this scene.*

Grumpop What size spanner were you looking for?

Natasha Fuck you.

Grumpop Is this how they build an engine on Goggle or Google or whatever it is? It's unconventional.

Natasha Why don't you fuck off?

Grumpop What's the principle? Throw enough fucking spanners at it and some of them will stick. Fix the fucking thing itself. You're not the only one who can swear. Comes with the territory. Fucking mechanics with no fucking manners and their fucking spanners. What size were you looking for? Metric, BSF or AF? Socket, ring or open-ended?

Natasha You think you're so... clever.

Grumpop They're just my tools, from my workshop. They know my hand and I do know the sizes just by looking. From a lifetime of habit. Routine work. Like you on the piano. Like you used to be.

Natasha Does that mean you're going to help?

Grumpop Throw everything on the floor?

Natasha Build the engine?

Grumpop No.

Natasha I don't know where to start.

Grumpop You're going to have to start sorting this lot out first. Did you hurt yourself?

Natasha No, why?

Grumpop There's blood on your... on Stevie's shirt.

Natasha It's nothing.

Grumpop You haven't even looked at it.

NATASHA looks everywhere but at her arms.

On the sleeve.

Natasha I must've scratched my arm on something.

Grumpop Let me have a look.

Natasha No. I'm alright.

Grumpop First-aid kit's on the floor behind you.

Natasha I'm sure it's nothing serious.

Grumpop A garage is not a very clean place you know. Might get infected.

Natasha If that's the worst that could happen...

Grumpop Are you on drugs?

Natasha What?

Grumpop You heard me. Are you shooting up?

Natasha Oh yeah, sure. You watch way too much TV, Grumps. What have you got down here I could shoot up with? A grease gun?

Grumpop I didn't say you did it down here. You did.

Natasha I'm not fucking shooting up, alright.

Grumpop Then let me look at your fucking arm?

A standoff.
NATASHA pulls up her sleeve and shows him where she has cut herself.

For Christ's sake, Tash. What's that about?

Natasha I cut myself.

Grumpop What with?

Natasha A Stanley knife. I found down here.

Grumpop Fucking hell. Did you change the blade?

Natasha Before or after?

Grumpop Okay. Be a smartarse then.

He starts to go.

Natasha I used a clean blade.

Grumpop At least that's intelligent. Why, Tash?

Natasha I don't know why. It stops me thinking. Sometimes there's so much going on in my head it's the only way I can smooth things out.

Grumpop Because I won't help you finish Stevie's car?

Natasha It's got nothing to do with you. I was doing it before I even thought of that.

Grumpop Does your mother know?

Natasha You have to promise me you won't tell her, or Dad. They've got enough to deal with already.

Grumpop I'm too old for this.

Natasha I'm trusting you.

Grumpop Why can't you just get a tattoo like everybody else?

Natasha You have to promise.

Grumpop Or what? You'll kill yourself?

Natasha It's what stops me from doing that.

Grumpop You're bullshitting me.

Natasha I googled it.

Grumpop Fucking Google.

Natasha Apparently it's normal. Sort of.

Grumpop Do they tell you the cure too?

Natasha They've got tips on how to stop. When you're ready. Venting is good.

Grumpop Venting?

Natasha Kind of what happened here. [*Pause.*] Telling someone when you feel like doing it is supposed to work too.

Grumpop I'll promise you if you promise me.

Natasha Okay.

Grumpop If we've got an agreement we have to shake on it.

Natasha Alright.

> *They shake hands. GRUMPOP keeps hold of her hand when she tries to pull away.*

Grumpop I promise I won't tell. I just need to see, in case I have to stitch it back on.

> *She shows him her left arm and he lets go of her hand.*

Natasha I never cut deep.

Grumpop Well, that's a mercy. But you're not going to cut without telling me first from now on.

Natasha I promise.

Grumpop Deal. You better put something on that arm. And do your venting somewhere else. It'll take a lot longer to clean this mess up than it did to make it.

Natasha What about Stevie's car, Pops?

Grumpop We didn't agree to that.

Natasha No, I know. I'm asking.

Grumpop Didn't you google it?

Natasha The real thing looks different. I didn't know what I was supposed to be looking at.

Grumpop The right model would be the place to start.

Natasha Can you tell me that at least? Please?

Grumpop [*pointing*] That's the workshop manual. For Stevie's car. This engine.

NATASHA picks up the manual from amongst the spanners.

Natasha Thanks.

Grumpop I suppose Google said if you keep your mind on other things...

Natasha Kind of. It might help.

Grumpop Yeah, well that's your mind. Not mine.

Natasha [*with a shrug*] I've got nothing to lose by trying. Except some blood.

Grumpop You'll find that spanners come in sets, arranged by size.

SCENE SHIFT

GRUMPOP with whiskey. During the scene he starts doing some work on the engine. He drops it off the chain and onto a mobile engine stand.

CHORUS 7: *The CHORUS play out GRUMPOP's first speculations of what was going on in the car, the kids having a good time. This loops as a piece of group-devised choreography based on things that happen in cars. The CHORUS leave at the end of the monologue.*

Grumpop Something happened in that car. Fucking hello! Something happened in that car? Let it go. There is no answer. What was he doing in the death seat? Riding shotgun? Don't ask.

If Tom knows, he's not talking. You know what happened in that car. Fletch told you. 'Mate, you don't want to come identify the body. You get me? I already done it. I had to look in his wallet. You get what I'm saying? Tell his folks, they don't need to see. That part's done. The only reason the driver survived—he had an airbag. Have a drink for me too.' Had a sixpack and a bottle of whiskey. Been on it ever since. Feel like a three-hundred-year-old man who's had his bones removed without anaesthetic. And you're preaching to the girl about taking drugs and slicing herself into pieces. Where do you get off?

SCENE SHIFT

TEXT MESSAGE [*with a photo or graphic image of the engine*]
  Heeelp! I need somebody. Help help meee
NATASHA is picking up spanners, sorting them.

Natasha I sent you a photo, Stevie. I need help. I'm going to finish your car. If you don't mind, that is. I know I haven't asked you. Grumps has got the grumps and said no. What he said first. Now he's at the he'll-think-about-it stage. I can tell. He helped you. I don't know why he won't help me. I sent the photo to Davo as well. He promised to come over.

> *DAVO is there.*

Davo Shit all over Texas, Tash.
Natasha Sorry, Davo, thought I would've sorted out these spanners by now.
Davo You want a hand.

> *He starts picking them up without any particular care.*

Natasha Grumps wants them sorted by size and make and type.
Davo I have to warn you I'm not really up on this stuff, Tash. It was Stevie's bag, engines and… shit, you know.
Natasha I've got the manual.
Davo That'll be a big, big help.
Natasha I kind of read it. It's a bit like a recipe in a foreign language. For boys.
Davo Yeah, some boys. Maybe. I reckon you've got the ingredients. Far as I can tell. Maybe enough for two engines.

Natasha So long as I end up with one.

Davo Tash, I'm more your get-in-the-car-and-drive kind of guy. If it doesn't go I call NRMA.

Natasha I can't really do that, can I? Anyway I want to do it myself. For Stevie.

Davo Sweet. I don't want to fuck it up.

Natasha I thought maybe together we could sort it out.

Davo Why doesn't your granddad just do it?

Natasha He gave me the manual, said I could use his tools but he doesn't really want to get involved.

Davo Jesus, Tash, he could probably do it in an afternoon. Blindfolded. Stevie said your granddad was dragging the chain.

Natasha Stevie said?

Davo Yeah. If Stevie'd been in his own car…

Natasha Yeah, if. Or if he'd gone home with you instead of Tom.

Davo My mum's car is only a Daihatsu.

Natasha Or if you hadn't been there I would have been in Tom's car as well.

Davo I'm glad you weren't, Tash. I'm glad I gave you a lift.

Natasha Everyone thinks they know what happened and they all talk about it. And when I walk up, they don't say anything. It's like it didn't happen. What do they think I'll do? Shatter?

Davo I'm not saying I'm some kind of hero. Stevie just told me that he had a blue with Grumps about getting it finished, that afternoon. He said he was sick of catching rides. If his car was going…

Natasha When will everyone stop doing that? Thinking if… if. If only. If only we could.

SCENE SHIFT

TEXT MESSAGE   if if if if if!!! If only

NATASHA becomes STEVIE. DAVO becomes GRUMPOP.

STEVIE works on the engine. He has to search around on the floor for the right tools.

Grumpop For crying out loud, Stevie, how many times do I have to tell you not to leave spanners all over the shop? If you put them back in the toolbox you always know where they are.

Stevie If I leave them on the floor I know where they are too.

Grumpop And you're always scrabbling round looking for the right tool rather than it being right to hand. You're the one that's in a hurry and you pay no attention to what I tell you.

Stevie All you keep telling me is to put the bloody spanners away when I'm in the middle of using them. You could give me a hand you know.

Grumpop If I did it how would you ever learn to do it?

Stevie I should've just paid a mechanic.

Grumpop You think mechanics are a more highly evolved species? Mate, most of them are knuckle draggers. You've got more faith in mechanics than I have. And in your mates' cars. Are they their own cars or their mum's cars? Have they had them apart? Do they know how to handle them?

Stevie What's it matter?

Grumpop Mum's car is the second car and it usually doesn't get the maintenance it should. And most parents think it's safe because it has a driver's airbag.

Stevie Isn't that a good thing?

Grumpop Only good for the driver. You know what I think about hopping in a car with one airbag. Don't ride shotgun.

Stevie In the passenger seat? You can't get in the back seat in your mate's car if it's just the two of you. It's not a taxi. I'd be crucified.

Grumpop Better than being a crash dummy.

Stevie My car doesn't have airbags.

Grumpop When the pilot is the only one with a parachute, don't get in the fucking plane. The point is don't count on safety gizmos to save you. Drive like your life depends on your driving. Like everyone's life does. You'll drive more carefully knowing that.

Stevie I wish I could drive the fucking thing at all.

Grumpop Hey, watch what you're doing. Don't take it out on the car.

Stevie I've had it with all your bullshit.

Grumpop Finish the engine, we'll put it back in and off you go.

Stevie Why don't I just pay you to do it?

Grumpop You just have to put in the time.

Stevie I trusted you, Grumpop. You said you'd help me and all you've done is give me grief. You helped me pull my car to bits when there was fuck-all wrong with it—

Grumpop It needed work done. We knew that when we bought it. You said you wanted to learn and I showed you what to do.

Stevie And you've just left me to put it back together on my own without lifting a finger except to wag it at me, do this, don't do that.

Grumpop So you'll remember. Putting it back together is just doing everything in reverse order to pulling it apart.

Stevie Fuck it. I'm reversing out of here. I don't think you ever wanted me to have that car. Not to drive anyway.

STEVIE goes.

Grumpop Stevie. Don't go off like that. Leaving everything half-baked and a trail of destruction in your wake. [*Calling after him*] You can't go through life like you've been shot out of a catapult.

SCENE SHIFT

A car shape made out of the tyres.

CHORUS 8: Two CHORUS members, dressed as lab technicians, manoeuvre two crash test dummies (two other CHORUS members) into the space. The dummies resist silently, playing dead, trying to escape. The dummies are strapped into the back seat.

NATASHA and GRUMPOP become crash dummies, LARRY and BOB.

Bob Mornin', Larry.

Larry Mornin', Bob.

Bob Who we mournin' today, Larry.

Larry Always the funny guy, Bob.

Bob What are we doin' today, Larry?

Larry We're gunna run this here v-hickle in a straight line at speed into that brick wall.

Bob Didn't we do that yesterday?

Larry I believe we did, Bob.

Bob Forgive my brain damage but didn't we die yesterday, Larry?

Larry I believe you're right, Bob.

Bob If we keep doing the same thing, Larry, how can we get a different result?

Larry You're not as brain damaged as you look, Bob. I believe we got a little surprise in store.

Bob Something you're not telling me, Larry.

Larry Let's just take her for a test run, Bob.

Bob Seatbelt, Larry.

Larry No need to buckle up, Bob. Seatbelts are for pussies.

And they're off with appropriate sound effects. CHORUS dummies also lean back with the acceleration.

Loud crash!

All smash forwards.

After the impact BOB is hanging mangled in his seatbelt. LARRY, the driver, is saved by an airbag.

Airbag. Oh man, did you see that? That was sick.

Bob I need a sickbag, Larry. I think I might be dead.

Larry Didn't even get a blood nose. We got to put one in every car, Bob.

Bob For the passenger?

Melanie Zanetti and Bob Baines in the 2010 NORPA production.
(Photo: David Young)

Larry Are you crazy, Bob? For the driver. I want to do that again.

Another sudden acceleration and crash as before. This time BOB looks around furtively.

Bob I've been thinking, Larry. Why don't we drive round that wall and head for an open paddock. Chuck a couple of u-ies, some double 360s. Get it to drift.

Larry That's not the sort of driving we save people from, Bob. We crash straight into things and t-bone each other all day long.

Bob Running into things is killing me. I want to learn to drive round things, and to stay out of trouble.

Larry Your career as a crash dummy would be over.

Bob That's the idea, Larry. Let's get out of here and do some living for a change.

Larry Too late, Bob. It's time to go again.

SCENE SHIFT

Back to the garage. GRUMPOP tidies away the tools as NATASHA enters.

TEXT MESSAGE you okay?

Grumpop Too late, Stevie, too late. I always wake up too late.

Natasha Hey, Grumpop. Sorry. I was going to finish doing that now.

Grumpop It's only right I should pick up my share.

Natasha I had dinner at Davo's place. It wasn't a casserole.

Grumpop He seems a nice kid. They're all nice kids, Stevie's mates. Maybe even Tom. He always seemed to hold back.

Natasha Does it even more now.

Grumpop All he has to do is apologise.

Natasha He's going to court.

Grumpop Has he said anything to you?

Natasha No, he avoids me. But he's not the only one.

Grumpop At least Davo still comes around.

Natasha He doesn't know anything about cars though.

Grumpop Didn't stop your father marrying your mother.

Natasha I'm not planning on marrying Davo.

Grumpop No, I know. I mean I'm glad your father did. Because now I've got you.

Natasha Are you okay, Grumpop?

Grumpop Yeah, I'm okay. I'm not fine, I'm not alright, that would be pretending too much. But I'm okay.

Natasha Have you been drinking?

Grumpop No. I've stopped. Maybe that's the problem. It's time I got a grip.

Natasha You've been working on the engine.

Grumpop No, not me, I just put it on the stand.

Natasha I took a photo before with my phone. It's different. [*Scrolling through her phone*] Oh. God.

Grumpop Yeah, could've been him.

Natasha No. It's Stevie.

Grumpop You seeing ghosts now?

Natasha On my phone. I don't remember taking this photo. It's from that night.

Grumpop The night of the crash?

Natasha Before. At the park. I was there. I wasn't supposed to be. But I didn't take this photo.

Grumpop You okay, Tash?

Natasha I just didn't know it was there. Or who took it. He looks so… Like he was just here.

Grumpop I swear I still see and hear him. Sometimes I think he's hidden my toothbrush or closed the bedroom door. It's probably good I'm giving up the whiskey.

Natasha He told Davo you'd had an argument. The same day.

Grumpop We did. That day. Before he went out. About the car. He said I wasn't helping him finish it. It would have been so easy for me to get it done. If I could have that afternoon again I could get it done. Even now. It would be so easy…

Natasha I don't want you to do it. You can't. I have to.

Grumpop There's still plenty for you to do. I couldn't have you starting on something that was left with things not done quite right.

Natasha Does that mean you're going to help me?

Grumpop I will when I see you've kept your promise.

Natasha Thanks, Grumps. I love you.

Grumpop I stuffed up, Tash.

Natasha Stevie was going anyway, wouldn't matter what you said.

Grumpop But I as good as put him in that car. I don't want to stuff up with you.

SCENE SHIFT

TEXT MESSAGE Very funny haha

NATASHA works on the engine through the following monologue and the next scene.

Natasha Who took the photo, Stevie? It was like being in a horror movie for a minute. Just without the music. Stopped my heart when I saw you. You've got Grumpop so spooked he agreed to help me do your car. Mum and Dad are still sitting in the kitchen. They used to be in bed at nine thirty. Now they sit up till all hours. Saying nothing. Or whispering to each other. Dad just came back from Sydney. The Minister put him on a Road Safety Advisory Panel as the Community Member. I think it was supposed to shut him up, but get this: Everyone else is an expert or a public servant. They all go round the table, say who they are, what university, what department, what they know. Then when it comes to Dad's turn, he says, 'Hi I'm Frank the father, how many of you have lost a child?' He just kills them.

SCENE SHIFT

TEXT MESSAGE hanging on

GRUMPOP and NATASHA.

Grumpop You'd tell me, wouldn't you?
Natasha What?
Grumpop If you were cutting yourself?
Natasha No.
Grumpop I thought we had an agreement, Tash. You promised me.
Natasha I promised I'd tell you before. If I felt like doing it.
Grumpop Right. Does that mean you have or you haven't?
Natasha You're not a very trusting person, Grumpop.
Grumpop That's probably why I'm still alive.
Natasha It's why you're easy to wind up.
Grumpop You haven't answered my question.
Natasha You're worse than the drug squad.

NATASHA pulls up her sleeve to show him her arm. She has a red post office rubber band on her wrist.

Grumpop Does that hurt more than cutting does?

NATASHA snaps the rubber band on her wrist.

Natasha Aargh—aaargh! You betcha. How'd you know?

Grumpop I googled it. Does that mean—?

Natasha No. You have to trust me, Grumpop. Okay? Or it's not going to work.

Grumpop Okay.

Natasha What do I do next?

Grumpop I told you about burying my brother.

Natasha All I remember is you said he was on the motorbike with two other blokes.

Grumpop Three on the bike. All pissed, but that's not what killed him. Jake had a bottle of whiskey in his shirt and when they came off he landed on it. Stabbed him in the heart. Black and White whiskey. I've tried a lot of whiskeys but I've never been able to drink that one. The other blokes walked away, one had a broken arm. Took the cops a day to track me down so I could identify him. I spewed and then I organised his funeral. Took four days before any other family turned up from Sydney. Then I had four years of wild living. Pills, drugs, booze, you name it.

Natasha You never mentioned drugs before.

Grumpop That bit shocked you, didn't it?

Natasha Suppose you were young once.

Grumpop Sex. Lots of. Girl under each arm. Girls. Plural. You better watch out for that Davo.

Natasha Now you're just being gross.

Grumpop Death is a great aphrodisiac.

Natasha I'm not doing drugs, booze or sex.

Grumpop I'm telling you because it took me four years.

Natasha For what?

Grumpop To wake up. One morning it occurred to me that four years of my life had gone in a blur. Like snap. And I was still spewing.

Natasha That's you. That's not me. I'm not like that.

Grumpop I learned one thing. There are no shortcuts. You do real time. No pills, no booze, no hanging on. It just prolongs the misery.

Natasha Is that what you think we're doing? Hanging on? To Stevie? Is that what I'm doing?

Grumpop You have to find your own answers.

Natasha Someone must have cut your heart out when your brother died.

Grumpop Maybe they did. But if you're building this engine to glorify Stevie just because he died, you're not thinking right. He had plenty of time to finish it himself.

Natasha If we're such losers you don't have to stay here, you know.

Grumpop Where else can I go?

The doorbell rings.

They both wait to see what happens. GRUMPOP puts down his tools.

The doorbell rings again.

Who is that? Some lost hugger with a casserole?

NATASHA sneaks a look to see who it is.

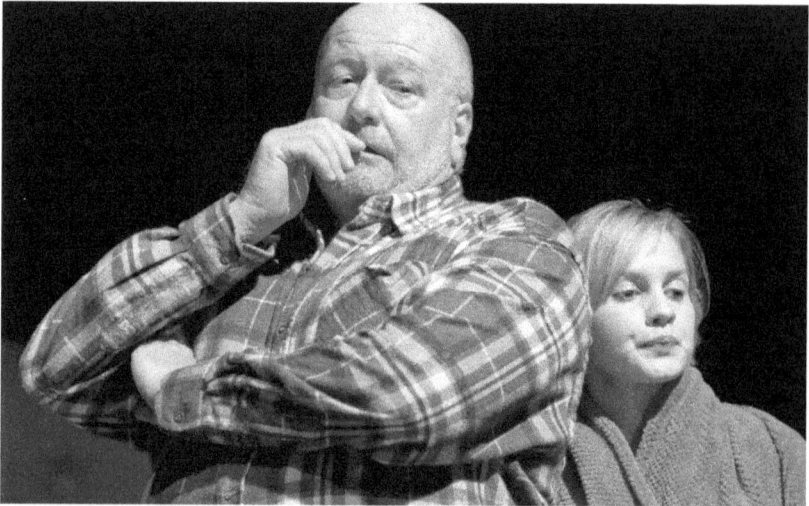

Bob Baines and Melanie Zanetti in the 2010 NORPA production. (Photo: David Young)

Natasha Father Donovan.

Grumpop Will your mum answer the door?

Natasha I don't want to see him.

Grumpop I suppose I better go and let him in then.

SCENE SHIFT

GRUMPOP becomes FATHER DONOVAN, waiting for someone to answer the door. NATASHA becomes MUM.

Mum It does get worse. It will probably get worse still. You hope that eventually you'll be able to cope without being frightened there will come a day I won't miss him. You are coping.

Father Donovan Hello. Anyone home?

Mum Oh, hello, Father. I wasn't expecting you.

Father Donovan I happened to be passing.

Mum Come in. [*Pause.*] Is it about Natasha going to school?

Father Donovan No no. I came to see you, Emily.

Mum Tash is going to school more now. Or she leaves home in her school uniform.

Father Donovan I've seen her there from time to time. [*Pause.*] Are you back into any kind of routine?

Mum For Tash?

Father Donovan For yourself as well.

Mum Frank goes to work. I haven't yet. I clean the house from top to bottom. Not his room though. You've probably never cleaned a house.

Father Donovan No, not really.

Mum Probably not your purpose.

Father Donovan No.

Mum Do you believe things happen for a purpose, Father?

Father Donovan It helps to believe if we want our lives to be meaningful.

Mum Cleaning never used to be my purpose before he…

Father Donovan I'm not going to say that Stevie is in a better place. Or tell you what the purpose of his life and death were, but nothing can diminish Stevie, nothing that made him Stevie can be lost.

Mum You think you are coping, till someone in the supermarket says, 'You must go on, for him. It's what he would have wanted.'

I just snapped. 'That is just so much crap. He would have wanted to go on, himself. He would have wanted to have his own life, just like your son.' I know they meant well, but I didn't care.

Father Donovan Do you not say his name.

Mum Less and less. [*Pause*.] I saw Tom at the supermarket too.

Father Donovan Tom? Who was driving?

Mum Tom. Who lived. And says nothing.

SCENE SHIFT

A CHORUS member becomes TOM, voiced by GRUMPOP/DONOVAN.

Mum Hello, Tom.

Tom Oh, hi, Mrs...

Mum Stevie's mum.

Tom Yeah, I wasn't... I know.

Mum Do I look that frightful? How are you?

Tom I'm okay now.

Mum Good. Natasha said you were going to a different school.

Tom That hasn't really worked out.

Mum What happened, Tom?

Tom None of the kids would talk to me and we've been getting death threats and all that stuff. I don't go where I know people if I can help it.

Mum No, Tom, what happened that night?

Tom It took three seconds. That's all.

Mum Three seconds?

Tom Three seconds.

Mum So you remember?

Tom I'm going to plead guilty.

Mum What are you guilty of, Tom, in those three seconds?

Tom The charges. For driving... I can't remember exactly what the solicitor said. I'll probably go to jail. I don't care. Maybe then everyone will be happy.

Mum I don't think so.

Tom Whatever it takes to get people off my back and leave me alone. I want it to end.

Mum It never ends. Not for us.

Tom I gotta go, Mrs...

Mum You used to call me Stevie's mum.

Tom Yeah. I'll be seeing you.

Mum Did the solicitors advise you not to talk to us, Tom?

Tom If I go to jail will that be enough?

Mum I'll still want to know, Tom, I'll always want to know.

Tom Do you wish I was dead, too?

Mum No, Tom. No.

Tom Sometimes I do.

Mum Yes.

Tom I gotta go. See you.

Mum You too, Tom.

> *TOM goes.*

SCENE SHIFT

MUM and FATHER DONOVAN.

Mum They all call me Stevie's mum. Called me.

Father Donovan He has a hard road to travel, that boy.

Mum Why couldn't he just say he was sorry?

Father Donovan Are you sorry for him?

Mum In my mind, maybe. Not in my heart.

Father Donovan Do you think he knows what happened and won't say?

Mum He killed three boys, Father. One of them mine.

Father Donovan You both know that. That's not what you were asking him.

Mum What is there to know about three seconds?

Father Donovan Do you think he should be punished?

Mum I can't ever forgive him.

Father Donovan Can you forgive yourself?

Mum That's so easy to say, Father.

Father Donovan I know. It doesn't make it any less true, or any less necessary.

> *Pause.*

Mum Can I get you a cup of tea, Father?

Father Donovan I don't want to put you to any trouble, Emily.

Mum In that case I won't then. [*Pause.*] I don't like for the doorbell to ring.

Father Donovan Sorry, Emily, I should have phoned first.

Mum I don't like the telephone much either.

Father Donovan That's understandable.

Mum When I hear it I can only remember that night.

> *MUM goes. FATHER DONOVAN is left sitting alone.*

SCENE SHIFT

TEXT MESSAGE Going for a drive home in 1 hour

Headland Park. The night of the crash. A phone rings.

GRUMPOP becomes STEVIE. NATASHA is MUM. Both on the phone.

Music from a car playing in the background. Heavy on the bass.

CHORUS 9: *The CHORUS is actively involved in the next sequence of scenes as Stevie's friends. Their dialogue is delivered energetically and rhythmically. They are having a great time.*

Mum Hi, Stevie.

Stevie Mum, watcha doin'?

Friends / Chorus Hi/ hi/ hello, Stevie's mum/ watcha doin', Mrs S?

Mum I'm wondering what the hell you're doing, Stevie.

Stevie Standing on the headland looking at the full moon jump out of the sea. It's gorgeous.

Friends / Chorus Gorgeous as/ you should see it/ Stevie's mum.

Mum You said you were going to Pete's place.

Stevie I did. Then we went for a drive. I left you a message.

Mum You said one hour almost an hour ago.

Stevie We went for a longer drive than we planned. It takes forty minutes to get here.

Mum Who's we?

Stevie Hey, who are we?

Friends / Chorus Depends who wants to know/ he's Stevie/ you're Pete/ no, I'm Pete/ you're Tom/ I'm me/ who's Dick?/ where's Harry?

> *Laughter.*

Mum Is Pete driving?

Stevie No-one's driving at the moment. We came in Tom's car.

Mum Are you drinking?

Stevie No, Mum. I give you my word. No alcohol. We're just having a good time.

Friends / Chorus No drugs/ no alcohol/ just a natural high.

Mum It sounds like a lot more of you.

Stevie There's a few other cars. Word gets around.

Mum Stevie, you know I don't like it when you do things like this.

Stevie Mum, we're looking at the moon.

Friends / Chorus And the chicky-babes/ and the racks/ woo-woo!/ shut up, you goose!

Mum I want you to keep your word and come home.

Stevie Don't worry, Mum. Everything's cool. I won't get dead.

Friends / Chorus Don't worry, Mrs S./ we'll bring Stevie-boy home/ don't worry, Stevie's mum/ safe and sound.

Mum Is Natasha with you?

Stevie Nope. Haven't seen her.

Mum Phone me when you're leaving. And make it soon.

Stevie I promise. We won't be long. Love you, Mum.

Friends / Chorus Love you, Mum/ Stevie's mum/ 'bye, Mrs S/ 'bye, Mum.

SCENE SHIFT

Headland Park. The night of the crash.

NATASHA is there. So is STEVIE.

Natasha Hey, Stevie, watcha doin'?

Stevie Watcha doin', Tash? When did you get here?

Natasha A few minutes ago. I came down with Rob and Bethany and Sarina.

Stevie Yeah?

Natasha What?

Stevie Bethany?

Natasha Yeah, Bethany.

Stevie You think I'm a chance?

Natasha You should ask her. I don't know.

Stevie Girls talk.

Natasha What, and boys don't?

Stevie So you do know.

Natasha I think she said you were hot.

Stevie Really?

Natasha Maybe she said cool. I can't remember.

Stevie You can be cruel, Tash.

Natasha You want me to ask her?

Stevie You got her number?

Natasha You know I have.

Stevie Well, give it to me then.

Natasha She's just over there you know.

Stevie We're about to go. Did Mum get hold of you?

Natasha I didn't answer it.

Stevie I said I hadn't seen you. You staying long?

Natasha Sarina wants to hang out for a bit.

Stevie We can probably give you a lift.

Natasha Got room for Bethany as well?

Stevie I have to ask Tom first.

Natasha I've got her number here.

STEVIE grabs her phone. She chases him but he eludes her easily.

Stevie Let me use yours.

Natasha No. Hey. Stevie.

Stevie Just a bit of fun.

Natasha Use your own.

Stevie Give her a surprise.

Natasha Bethany's going to think I put you up to this.

Stevie I'll come and get you when we're leaving.

SCENE SHIFT

NATASHA alone.

Natasha That's when you took the photo, isn't it, Stevie? With my phone. And sent it to Bethany. I wasn't going to be anywhere near her when she got your message. That'd be too embarrassing. She's never said anything about it. Lucky you didn't offer her a lift. All she did was smile when I told her I was leaving that night.

SCENE SHIFT

STEVIE's phone rings. It's MUM.
NATASHA becomes MUM again.

Stevie Mum, watcha doin'?

Mum I'm about to get in the car to come down and get you.

Stevie No way. Come on, Mum. That would not be cool.

Mum You said you'd be home by now, Stevie.

Stevie Mum, I've just rounded everyone up. We're about to get in the car.

Friends / Chorus Getting in the car now, Stevie's mum/ everything's cool/ in the car.

Mum I'm worried about you.

Stevie Then don't. I'm safe. Nothing's happening, okay? We're leaving.

Friends / Chorus Leaving now/ get in the car/ safe as, Stevie/ safe as /very okay.

Mum I'd feel a lot better if I drove down and picked you up.

Stevie You don't have to. 'Cause I won't be here. Tom's waiting for me, now.

Mum Stevie, I'd rather you stayed put until I get there.

Stevie If you're worried about me being safe, Mum, the others will probably wait too, till you get here. They won't just leave me.

Mum Call me when you're on the road.

Stevie In five minutes. Love you, Mum.

Friends / Chorus Love you, Mum/ Stevie's mum/ 'bye, Mrs S./ 'bye, Mum.

SCENE SHIFT

The sound of the car driving out of the carpark and leaving. Horns at the tyre squeal.

TEXT MESSAGE On the way see you soon

Stevie & Friends / Chorus Mum/ mum/ mum/ mum…

> *This merges into the sound of the car's engine*
>
> ***CHORUS 10****: This movement routine/choreography is as close to a real crash as is possible. It is similar to the 'having a good time' version seen before, but now it ends with a crash and broken bodies. It is the last three seconds and the immediate aftermath stretched out to sixty seconds or so.*
>
> *Silence.*
>
> *CHORUS end up thrown about in the car.*

SCENE SHIFT

TEXT MESSAGE sorry mum missed your call home in 5 :)
NATASHA and MUM.

Natasha I wasn't even home when it happened. I would've been in Davo's car still, on the way. Mum was waiting when I got home. First thing she said—

Mum I thought it might be Stevie.

Natasha No, only me. Did he phone you?

Mum Yes. Something you could learn to do.

Natasha Sorry, Mum. Had my phone on silent.

Mum What good's that? Where were you?

Natasha We went to the Club after the movies. I wouldn't have been able to hear you anyway.

Mum Aren't you underage?

Natasha Depends who's on the door.

Mum No, you're either underage or not. You're underage.

Natasha Okay, we shouldn't have gone. I won't do it again.

Mum Please don't. Stevie should be home soon. How did you get home?

Natasha Davo gave me a lift home.

Mum Davo's nice.

Natasha He just gave me a lift, that's all.

Mum It's nice all the same.

Natasha He's not my boyfriend.

Mum Fine. All I said was he's nice. I like him.

Natasha Then the phone rings. It's in Mum's hand and she jumps like she's been electrocuted. You're all she's been thinking about because when she answers she's expecting it to be you.

Mum Stevie?… Sorry… Yes it is… Is anybody hurt?…

Natasha Then I get a text message and I just start saying, Mum. Mum. Mum. I forgot she was on the phone.

TEXT MESSAGE Stevie in accident police won't tell anything

Natasha I look up and I see that she knows too. Because she's staring at the phone in her hand and she's completely bloodless. Is Stevie alright?

Mum They said they'd call back. When they know.

Natasha He'll be alright. He'll ring us. He knows you'll worry. Mum tried your number over and over. Dad was away. It was just Mum and me. She puts the phone down and her hand is shaking.

Mum They won't get through if I'm on the phone the whole time.

Natasha I tell her. Mum, I was there. Down at the park. I'm sorry. I should have told you.

Mum I don't have time for that now, Natasha.

Natasha I saw Stevie before he left there. He was fine. And it's like at that moment we both know. Mum got up and did the ironing. That's when I first sent you that text.

TEXT MESSAGE Come home Stevie please come home

SCENE SHIFT

NATASHA is cutting herself.

Natasha I can't go in your room anymore. I don't know why. I can't even bring myself to look in the door. There's a pair of your shoes there under the desk. Empty. There's still a pair of your thongs in the laundry. Sometimes I just stare at them. I try to imagine you wearing them and I can't. Empty thongs, Stevie. Empty shoes. I've never thought of shoes being empty before. In shops but not when they belong to someone. There are holes everywhere now. At the table, in the car, on the couch. No-one else sits there. Empty holes. On the stairs even there's a Stevie hole. In the school cricket team. And your clothes are empty too. That's why I can't go in your room. Your room is empty.

> *GRUMPOP enters.*

Grumpop Natasha, what the hell are you doing? You promised you'd tell me. You promised.

Natasha I couldn't find you.

Grumpop You promised me.

Natasha I tried to tell you but you weren't here.

Grumpop I'm sorry, Tash. This is not going to be my fault. Emily!

Natasha No, you promised.

Grumpop Only as long as you kept yours. You didn't. Emily!

45

SCENE SHIFT

GRUMPOP and MUM.

Mum What is it? What's wrong?

Grumpop Every damn thing is what's wrong. It's a totally stuffed-up situation. From arsehole to breakfast time. I can't do this anymore.

Mum Dad, what are you talking about? What's happened?

Grumpop That's just it. Nothing's happened. Everything's stuck. On that one night. I can't live like this, Em. You can't go on living like this. The place is a mess and it's getting worse every day. There's ironing everywhere. Frank's paperwork is piled up like a roadblock from God only knows when.

Mum It's all from the Road Safety Committee.

Grumpop I cook meals but no-one wants to eat, or you all come and go when you feel like it. No-one sits at the table anymore. You shop at Coles or the IGA when I ask you to get stuff from ALDI.

Mum No-one asked you to cook. Don't cook.

Grumpop What would you do then?

Mum We'd survive.

Grumpop Survival's not good enough. Survival isn't living. It's time you started looking at what's going on around here, Emily.

Mum I don't need you to tell me what's happened here, Dad. We're all just doing the best we can. Do you think we can just forget about Stevie?

Grumpop You idolised Stevie. You always did. But he wasn't a saint. He was probably the cheekiest kid I've ever come across and he could be a bastard. Stevie knew how to get his own way. You just don't remember the bad things he did.

Mum If things here aren't to your liking, Dad, you don't have to stay. No-one asked you to stay.

Grumpop I stayed for Natasha. She needed someone while you and Frank were naturally… There's nothing right about Stevie dying. We can ask all we want and we'll never know how, and even if we did it would make no difference. Stevie's gone. You have another child, you know. Do you have any idea what's going on with Tash?

Mum You always knew how to twist the knife.

Grumpop That's what Natasha's using, Em. A knife. On herself.

Mum Natasha's doing what?

Grumpop Cutting herself. I promised Tash I wouldn't tell you but I can't bear to watch it happen. That's what I'm telling you. You have to deal with it.

Mum Natasha.

Grumpop If you're up for sorting that with Tash, I will get out of your hair and move back to my own place.

Mum That would probably be best.

Grumpop I've been here too long, just getting in the way.

Mum Thanks for telling me.

Grumpop Do you blame me for getting Stevie interested in cars and what happened?

Mum No, Dad, why would I think that?

Grumpop Because I do.

Mum Boys love cars. Stevie loved cars. That's not a bad thing. He loved you too, Pops. Stevie knew you wouldn't do anything to harm him.

Grumpop I'm sorry about what I said.

Mum Are you?

Grumpop No. Probably just as well I'm going.

Mum I'd better go find Natasha.

SCENE SHIFT

NATASHA alone.

Natasha I'm here, Mum. I'm still here.

SCENE SHIFT

MUM in Stevie's room. Starts to fold his clothes and pack them up.
DAD at the door. Disconcerted by what she is doing.

Dad The Committee's recommendations have finally gone to the Minister.

Mum At least you'll be home more.

Dad Cabinet has to pass them. We'll have to keep the pressure on.

Mum Meaning you.

Dad I'll see it through to the end.

He offers her a pill. She refuses.

Mum I haven't been taking them.

47

Dad Since when?

Mum For a while now.

>   *She gives him the receptacle of pills she hasn't taken.*

Dad I tried to stop taking them but they seem to soak up the tears.

Mum I've been staying awake, waiting, hoping Stevie would come to me. He hasn't. Stevie isn't coming back.

Dad No. Nothing will bring him back.

>   *He tries to put the doona around her shoulders.*

Mum Don't comfort me. I don't need that right now.

>   *She takes the doona from him and folds it up.*

Dad We've both become someone else.

Mum We look the same, we sound the same, the same but different.

Dad Does that make us strangers?

Mum This is our life now. It's not fixable, it'll never be fixable, but maybe it'll heal over and no-one will know or notice.

Dad We still have to fight to make driving safer for kids. But after that, I can't go on living the same life.

Mum Do you think there is an 'us' in the future?

Dad In truth I don't know what to do. I can't see, or understand, or bear to think about it. I just have to beat the bastards who say things like, 'If a plane had fallen out of the sky that day, no-one would've heard of your boys'.

Mum I know you'll win.

Dad We can't win. Any change in the law is an admission that the previous laws were inadequate and that Stevie could still be alive. Are you saying there's no 'us' anymore?

Mum Now we're starting a new life. Natasha, you, me. We have to find what hope and happiness we can. Together and apart. One thing, Stevie will always be with us.

SCENE SHIFT

CHORUS 11: The CHORUS members take their leave. MUM gives one of them the bag of Stevie's clothes she has folded and packed. A look between the CHORUS and MUM and DAD, and then they are gone.

SCENE SHIFT

NATASHA and GRUMPOP.

Natasha Do you think Stevie would've let me drive his car?
Grumpop Is it still his car?
Natasha It will always be Stevie's car, no matter what.
Grumpop If he wouldn't let you, Tash, I'd have something to say about it.
Natasha I thought you were going to stop telling people what they should do, Grumps?
Grumpop Yeah, well. It's not like he left it in drivable condition.
Natasha I've been thinking about what you said. About why I wanted to finish it.
Grumpop I've been thinking too, that I should keep my mouth shut.
Natasha I want the car, Grumps. I'll probably always think of it as Stevie's car, but I want it for myself. He'll always be in it, but so would you be.
Grumpop If I help you finish it?
Natasha Even if you don't. I'll know you worked on it with Stevie because you cared about him and his car.
Grumpop I care about you too, Tash. I just couldn't face it anymore. Probably why I broke my promise and told your mum you were cutting yourself first chance I got.
Natasha I broke my promise too, Grumps. Mum was always going to know. I would've had to tell her if you didn't.
Grumpop That's not a good reason. I gave you my word and I didn't really give you a second chance.
Natasha If you can tell me a good mechanic. I have some money saved and they might let me pay it off.
Grumpop So you're not going to give me a second chance then?
Natasha Not if it's going to upset you.
Grumpop You could at least ask me.
Natasha I'd love you to but...
Grumpop But what?
Natasha I'd want to do it with you.
Grumpop I wasn't going to do it on my own.
Natasha That's what I'm asking, Grumps. Please. It's for me.
Grumpop Okay. But...

Natasha But what?

Grumpop Does that mean you forgive me or are you just exploiting me because I'm cheap.

Natasha I did hate you but I'm over that now. And you don't come cheap, Grumps, you're really hard work.

Grumpop We've got a deal then.

They shake hands. This time NATASHA won't let his hand go.

Natasha You have to promise to teach me to drive it as well.

Grumpop I knew there'd be a catch. You give someone a hand they take your arm.

Natasha So I stop being scared.

Grumpop I reckon Stevie would be chuffed you want to drive his car.

Natasha It will always be Stevie's car.

Grumpop It won't take us long now, to get this engine started.

SCENE SHIFT

Light only on the engine. As the light fades we hear the engine start. It revs loudly.

THE END

www.currency.com.au

Visit Currency Press' website now to:

- Buy your books online
- Browse through our full list of titles, from plays to screenplays, books on theatre, film and music, and more
- Choose a play for your school or amateur performance group by cast size and gender
- Obtain information about performance rights
- Find out about theatre productions and other performing arts news across Australia
- For students, read our study guides
- For teachers, access syllabus and other relevant information
- Sign up for our email newsletter

The performing arts publisher

www.ingramcontent.com/pod-product-compliance
Lightning Source LLC
Chambersburg PA
CBHW041934090426
42744CB00017B/2056